multicultural and multiracial

Thank you for purchasing a Joanie Boney book!

Printed in the USA

About the Author: Joanie Boney Books are multicultural and multiracial reflecting the true America.

Illustrator: Natasha Kostovska

U-Impact Publishing LLC

I would like to know how much you liked my book so please leave a review.

MY FOREVER HOME

Written by: Joanie Boney

Illustrations: Natasha Kostovska

Winston wanted to look his best so he groomed himself, making sure to get his ears, head, and chest. He had the blackest shiniest fur, and even blacker whiskers. He needed to look remarkable.

The human came and took Winston out of the kennel and placed him into the play area, he meowed his thank you and sat down.

"Hey, Mittens!" Winston hollered to a white kitten with gray paws. "I feel lucky about today."

"I hope so! You haven't been picked how many times now?" Mittens asked, feeling bad for her friend. "Thirteen times, but who's counting." Winston snickered.

Just then, the door opened and a family with two children walked in. "Time to work the charm." Winston said. Winston let out a sweet purr as he strolled over to the kids and rolled onto his back.

He kicked up his paws as he nuzzled into the little boy's knee. Without warning, the boy jumped to his feet. "Mom! That cat just gave me bad luck, didn't it?!" The boy screamed as he stumbled away.

Winston slowly rolled to his feet and stared at the kids as they slipped past him. He whimpered at them, which only made the family more scared.

"Why are they always scared of me?" Winston asked Mittens, which sounded like a meow to the family. "It's not fair... You're such an awesome kitten!" Mittens exclaimed, meowing to the humans.

Mittens ran over to Winston, not wanting to be separated. "Oh no, don't get close to the bad kitten!" Their dad quickly scooped up Mittens as the family exited the room.

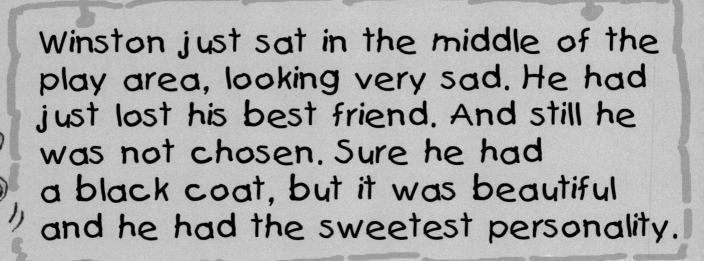

Winston just sat in the middle of the play area, looking very sad. He had just lost his best friend. And still he was not chosen. Sure he had a black coat, but it was beautiful and he had the sweetest personality.

He slumped over to the door and waited until he had to go back into his kennel.

The next day, he was plunked back into the play area as another family came to choose. He was on his best behaviour and was determined to be chosen. He waited with his most favorite toy until the family arrived.

Winston quickly galloped towards them and nudged his toy at them. But just like last time, the kids ran away and the parents told them he was bad luck.

Winston slumped away and sat in the corner until they left with another kitten. On and on it went until he was the only one left from his group.

As another batch of kittens arrived, he stood even less chance of getting picked. Of course they would pick a colorful kitten over an older black kitten; practically a cat by then!

He couldn't help that he wasn't grey or white, he was who he was. Winston knew he was an amazing kitten and could make any family happy if he was given the chance, but everyone just kept thinking he was bad luck.

And this time a family came in. As Winston walked up to the Dad, Mom quickly picked him up and gave him, a big hug.

The kids quickly ran over and they all started petting Winston with lots of love and affection.

Winston was so happy. He let out a big meow which said this is my forever family.

me

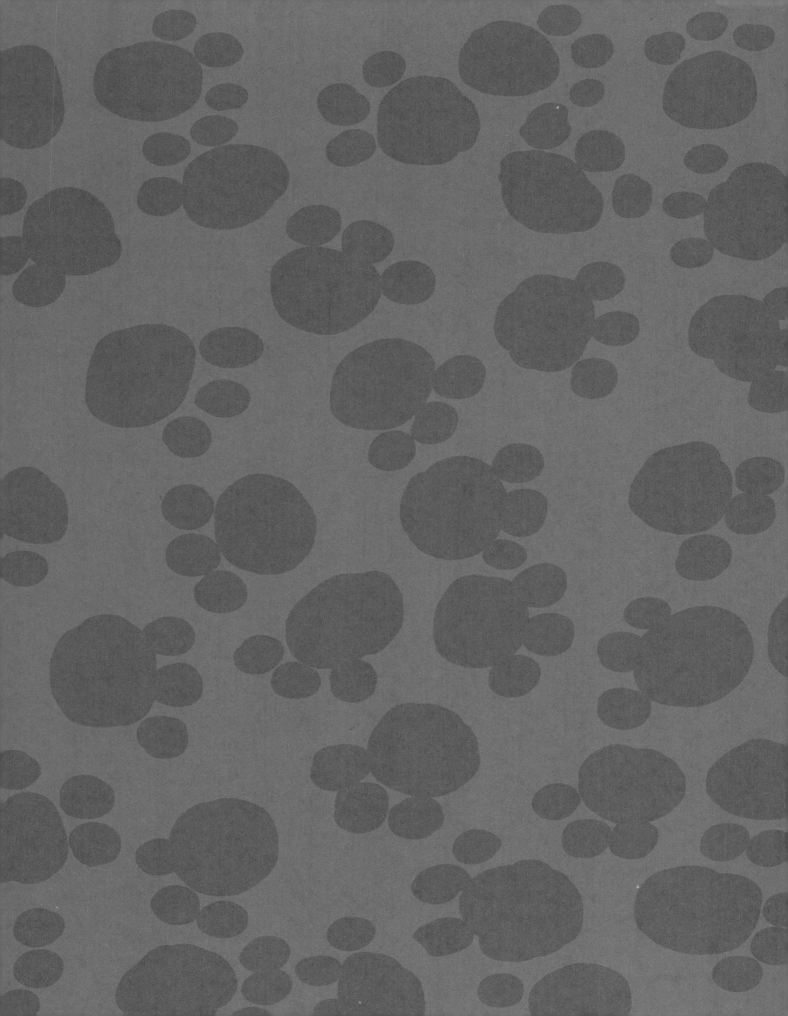

Made in the USA
Middletown, DE
23 March 2022

63108447R00031